Table Of Contents

Introduction

Definition of TikTok and Instagram

TikTok and Instagram are two of the most popular social media platforms today with millions of active users worldwide. Both platforms offer unique features that make them ideal for social media advertising, but they also have their pros and cons.

TikTok is a video sharing app that allows users to create short videos that are typically 15 to 60 seconds long. It's especially popular with Gen Z and millennial audiences, making it an ideal platform for brands targeting younger audiences. TikTok's algorithm is also known for its ability to make videos go viral quickly, which can greatly increase the reach of advertising campaigns. Instagram, on the other hand, is a photo and video sharing app with a larger user base than TikTok, with more than a billion active users. Offers a wider range of content formats, including photos, videos and Instagram stories. Instagram is popular among all age groups, making it a universal platform for brands to reach large audiences.

When it comes to social media advertising, TikTok and Instagram offer many advertising options. TikTok offers in-feed video ads, branded hashtag challenges, and brand takeover announcements. On the other hand, Instagram offers photo and video ads, Instagram story ads, and carousel ads.

One of the main advantages of TikTok ads is the ability to distribute videos quickly. This means that even small businesses with a budget can reach millions of viewers with a well-planned TikTok campaign. Instagram's algorithm, on the other hand, is more focused on showing users content from accounts they already follow, which can make it harder for new brands to attract.

However, Instagram offers more advertising options than TikTok, including carousel ads that allow brands to display multiple products in a single ad.

Instagram also allows brands to target specific audiences based on interests, behaviors and demographics, which can help maximize the impact of advertising campaigns.

Bottom line: TikTok and Instagram offer unique advantages and disadvantages for social media advertising. Brands should carefully consider their audience and advertising goals before deciding which platform to use. Ultimately, a successful social media campaign depends on creating engaging and relevant content that resonates with your target audience, regardless of the platform you're using.

Importance of social media advertising

Social media has become an integral part of our lives and has changed the way we communicate, share information and do business. Social media advertising has become a powerful tool for companies to connect with their target audience and promote their products or services. In this subsection, we discuss the importance of social media advertising and how it can be used for business growth.

In particular, social media advertising is an effective way to reach a larger audience. Social media platforms like TikTok and Instagram have millions of active users and businesses can use these platforms to promote their products or services to a wider audience. With the right targeting options, businesses can reach their ideal customers and increase their visibility.

Second, advertising on social networks is cost-effective. Traditional advertising methods, such as television commercials or billboards, can be expensive and may not fit into the budget of small businesses. However, social media advertising offers affordable options that even small businesses can afford. With a limited budget, businesses can create targeted ads and reach a wider audience. Third, social media advertising allows for precise targeting.

Social media platforms like TikTok and Instagram offer targeting options that help businesses reach their ideal customers. Businesses can target their ads based on demographics, interests, behavior and location, among other things. This precise targeting ensures that businesses reach the right audience and increase the likelihood of conversions.

Fourth, social media advertising allows you to monitor performance in real time. Social media platforms have built-in analytics tools that allow businesses to monitor the performance of their ads in real time. This allows businesses to tailor campaigns and optimize ads for better performance.

In conclusion, social media advertising is an important tool for companies that want to increase their visibility, reach a wider audience and grow their business. With the right targeting options, affordable pricing, and real-time performance tracking, businesses can use social media advertising for maximum impact. TikTok and Instagram offer unique benefits for social media advertising, and businesses should carefully consider which platform best suits their needs.

Purpose of the book

This book aims to provide a comprehensive guide to using TikTok and Instagram for social media advertising. With the rise of social media platforms, businesses need to use these platforms to reach their target audience. TikTok and Instagram are two of the most popular social media platforms with millions of users worldwide. Therefore, it is very important for companies to understand the pros and cons of advertising on these platforms.

This book is dedicated to answering all your questions about TikTok and Instagram ads. It covers a variety of topics, including the benefits of social media advertising, the differences between TikTok and Instagram, the types of ads available on these platforms, and best practices for advertising on each platform. It also provides tips on how to create engaging content that resonates with your target audience.

The book is written in simple, easy-to-understand language, making it accessible to everyone, regardless of their social media experience. Whether you're a small business owner, marketer, or influencer, this book will provide you with invaluable insight into the world of social media advertising.

Also, this book is not intended for any specific platform. It provides an objective analysis of the pros and cons of TikTok and Instagram advertising to help readers make informed decisions based on their advertising goals and audience.

Overall, Pros and Cons of TikTok and Instagram Ads: A Must Read for Everyone is an essential guide for anyone looking to harness the power of social media advertising to grow their business or personal brand. This book will give you a better understanding of how to create effective social media ads that drive engagement and conversions on TikTok and Instagram.

Overview of the pros and cons of TikTok and Instagram advertising

Social media advertising has become an essential part of the marketing strategies of companies of all sizes. Platforms like TikTok and Instagram allow businesses to reach large audiences and promote their products or services more effectively. However, choosing between TikTok and Instagram ads can be a challenge. Each platform has its pros and cons, and understanding them is critical to making the right decision.

TikTok is a relatively new platform that has quickly become popular among a younger audience. It offers short video content that is easy to create and share. Many businesses have started using TikTok to promote their products and services, and the platform offers a number of benefits. First, TikTok has a huge user base, making it a great platform to reach a large audience. In addition, the platform's algorithm promotes content based on engagement, which means that if a video is engaging, it will likely reach more viewers. TikTok also offers unique advertising opportunities such as sponsored hashtags and challenges that can help businesses promote their products. However, TikTok also has some drawbacks. First, the platform's user base is relatively young, which means it may not be suitable for companies targeting an older audience. Additionally, the platform's advertising options can be more expensive than other social media platforms, making it less affordable for small businesses.

On the other hand, Instagram is a more established platform with a larger user base. It offers various advertising options such as photo and video ads, Instagram stories, and sponsored posts. Instagram also has more targeting options to help businesses reach specific audiences more effectively. In addition, Instagram's analytics tools are more advanced and allow businesses to more accurately track the success of their campaigns.

However, Instagram also has some drawbacks. Instagram's algorithm prioritizes content from highly engaging accounts, making it difficult for small businesses to get exposure. Also, the cost of Instagram ads can be quite high, making them less affordable for small businesses. Bottom line: TikTok and Instagram offer unique advantages and disadvantages to social media advertising. Choosing between the two platforms depends on your company's target audience, budget, and marketing goals. Understanding the pros and cons of each platform is essential to making an informed decision and creating an effective social media marketing strategy.

TikTok Advertising

Overview of TikTok advertising

TikTok is an app that has grown exponentially in recent years and has over 1 billion active users worldwide. It is a social media platform that allows users to create short videos and share them with the world. TikTok is a platform that has caught the attention of young people looking for a fun and engaging way to express themselves. The platform has become a hotbed for advertising, with brands looking for ways to tap into TikTok's massive audience.

TikTok's advertising platform is unique and offers a variety of advertising options for brands. The platform has four main ad formats: feed ads, brand takeovers, hashtag challenges and brand effects. Feed ads are short videos that appear in a user's feed and blend in with other content on the platform. Brand takeovers are full-screen ads that appear when a user opens your app and are great for making a good first impression. Hashtag challenges are a great way for brands to connect with consumers and encourage them to create content around a particular theme or topic. Brand Effects are AR filters and effects that users can apply to their videos and are a great way to increase brand awareness. One of the main advantages of TikTok advertising is that the platform has a highly engaged user base. TikTok users spend an average of 52 minutes a day on the app and are always looking for new and interesting content to engage with. This means brands have an engaging audience willing to engage with and share their content with others.

Another benefit of advertising on TikTok is that the platform's algorithm is designed to promote engaging and relevant content. This means that brands have a better chance of reaching their target audience on TikTok than other social media platforms. In conclusion, TikTok is a powerful advertising platform and offers brands a variety of advertising options. With a highly engaged user base and an algorithm that promotes engaging content, TikTok is a platform worth considering for brands looking to reach a younger audience.

However, before making a final decision, it is necessary to weigh the pros and cons of TikTok ads compared to other social media platforms like Instagram.

Advantages of TikTok advertising

TikTok has become one of the most popular social media platforms in recent years with millions of users worldwide. Therefore, it has become an increasingly popular platform for businesses to advertise their products and services. In this subsection, we explore the benefits of TikTok advertising and why it has become a popular business choice.

One of the main advantages of TikTok ads is reach. TikTok has a huge user base of millions of active users worldwide. This means that companies can reach a large audience with their advertising campaigns. Additionally, TikTok's algorithm is designed to promote popular and engaging content, which means businesses can get their ads seen by a wider audience.

Another benefit of TikTok ads is engagement. TikTok is a highly engaging platform with users spending an average of 52 minutes a day on the app. This means that businesses can create eye-catching ads that grab the attention of their target audience. In addition, TikTok's unique features such as filters, music, and effects allow businesses to create creative and engaging ads.

TikTok ads are also convenient. Advertising on TikTok is relatively cheap compared to other social media platforms. This means that businesses can create and display ads on TikTok without spending a lot of money. In addition, TikTok offers a variety of advertising options such as in-feed ads, brand endorsements, and sponsored hashtags, which means businesses can choose the advertising option that best suits their needs and budget. Finally, advertising on TikTok offers a unique opportunity to reach a younger audience. TikTok is particularly popular with a younger audience, as many users are under the age of 30. This means that businesses can use TikTok ads to reach this audience that may be difficult to reach through other advertising channels.

Finally, advertising on TikTok offers many advantages, including reach, engagement, affordability, and a unique opportunity to reach a younger audience. As TikTok continues to grow in popularity, businesses need to look at it as a viable advertising platform to effectively reach their target audience.

Targeted audience

When it comes to social media advertising, it's important to target the right audience. Your ad can be visually appealing and innovative, but if it doesn't reach the right people, it won't be effective. That's why it's so important to understand your target audience, whether you're advertising on TikTok or Instagram.

TikTok is known for its younger users, most of whom are between the ages of 16 and 24. This demographic is more open to trying new things and more likely to engage with content that appeals to them. If your product or service is aimed at a younger audience, TikTok ads can be a great way to reach them.

On the other hand, Instagram has a larger user base with people of all ages using the platform. However, Instagram's largest age group is 25-34, making it a great platform for millennials. Also, Instagram is known for its visual appeal, so if your product or service is visually driven, Instagram advertising may be the way to go.

It's important to note that both platforms offer targeting options beyond just age. You can target users based on interests, behavior, location, and even the specific hashtags they use. This way you can be even more specific to your target audience and ensure that your ad reaches the right people.

When choosing your TikTok and Instagram ads, it's important to think about your product or service and who your ideal customer is. If you're not sure where to start, market research can help you better understand who your target audience is and where they spend their time online.

Ultimately, targeting the right audience is key to the success of your social media advertising campaign. By understanding your audience and using the targeting options available on TikTok and Instagram, you can ensure that your ad reaches the right people and delivers the results you want.

High engagement rates

High engagement rates

One of the most important factors any brand or business should consider when deciding which platform to advertise on is the engagement rate. Engagement rates measure the number of clicks, comments, shares, and other interactions with a post. The higher the engagement rate, the more likely the post will be seen by a wider audience and the more effective the advertising campaign will be.

When it comes to engagement rates, TikTok and Instagram have their strengths. TikTok is known for its high engagement levels, with users spending an average of 52 minutes a day on the app. This means that brands have great potential to reach a large and engaged audience on TikTok. In addition, the platform's algorithm is designed to display content that will be of greater interest to users, meaning that high-quality, engaging content is more likely to be seen by a wider audience.

Instagram also has a high level of engagement, especially when it comes to visual content such as photos and videos. In fact, Instagram has been found to have the highest engagement of any social media platform, with an average engagement rate of 4.7%. This means that brands that can create visually appealing and engaging content on Instagram are likely to get a high return on their advertising investment. However, it's important to note that engagement rates can vary greatly depending on a number of factors, including industry, target audience, and the type of content being shared. For example, a brand targeting fashion or beauty might see higher engagement rates on Instagram, while a brand targeting a younger audience might see better results on TikTok.

Finally, when deciding which platform to advertise on, it's important to consider not only overall engagement rates, but also the specific needs and goals of your brand or business. Understanding the strengths and weaknesses of TikTok and Instagram will help you make an informed decision about which platform best suits your advertising needs.

Viral potential

In today's digital age, viral content has become the holy grail of social media marketing. With the rise of platforms like TikTok and Instagram, businesses and brands alike are constantly looking for ways to create content that goes viral and reaches millions within hours. We call this phenomenon "viral potential".

Viral potential is the content's ability to quickly become popular and widely shared across social media platforms. It's every marketer's dream, but not everyone can make it happen. This requires creativity, time and a deep understanding of your audience. TikTok and Instagram are two social media platforms that offer different types of content and audiences. TikTok is known for its short videos and fashion challenges, while Instagram offers a mix of photos, videos and stories. Both platforms have their own unique features that can help increase viral potential.

One of the keys to achieving viral potential is creating shareable content. This means creating content that people want to share with their friends and followers. It can be a funny video, an inspirational quote or a beautiful picture. Content should evoke emotion and connect with the audience in a meaningful way.

Another important factor is time. Publishing content at the right time can make a difference. For example, posting a Halloween-themed video in November might not get as much attention as posting in October. Understanding your audience's behavior and preferences is key to determining the best time to post.

Both TikTok and Instagram offer features that can help increase your viral potential. For example, TikTok's "Jums" page algorithm is designed to show users popular and trending content. This means that if your content is engaging and resonates with your audience, it can reach millions of people.

Similarly, Instagram's Explore page shows users content similar to what they've liked or worked on before. This means that if your content is relevant and targeted to your audience, it can reach a wider audience.

In conclusion, viral potential is the key to success in social media marketing. Creating shareable content, posting it at the right time, and using the features of TikTok and Instagram can help your content go viral. However, achieving viral potential is not guaranteed and requires a deep understanding of your audience and their behavior.

Disadvantages of TikTok advertising

TikTok is an incredibly popular social media platform that has taken the world by storm. With millions of daily active users, it's no surprise that businesses are turning to TikTok ads as a means of reaching their target audience. However, like any advertising platform, using TikTok for advertising also has some drawbacks.

One of the biggest downsides to TikTok ads is that it can be difficult to target specific audiences. Unlike other social media platforms like Facebook or Instagram, TikTok does not have robust targeting options. This means that advertisers have to rely on broad targeting options that may not reach their target audience.

Another downside to advertising on TikTok is that it can be expensive. While there are some affordable options like influencer marketing, advertising directly on TikTok can be expensive. This is especially true for businesses that are just starting out and have a limited advertising budget.

TikTok also has a younger audience than other social media platforms. While this may appeal to some advertisers, it can also be a disadvantage for businesses targeting an older demographic. Advertising on TikTok may not be the most effective way to reach an older audience.

Another disadvantage of TikTok ads is that it can be difficult to create engaging content. TikTok is a platform that revolves around creativity and entertainment, so companies need to create content that is both entertaining and relevant to their brand. This can be a challenge for companies that are new to the platform or don't have the resources to create quality content. In general, advertising on TikTok has its advantages, but also a number of disadvantages. Before investing in TikTok advertising, businesses should carefully consider whether TikTok is the right platform for their advertising needs and weigh the pros and cons.

Limited targeting options

While TikTok and Instagram offer powerful advertising platforms, there are some limitations to their targeting options that advertisers should be aware of.

One of the major limitations of both platforms is the inability to target specific keywords or phrases. This means that advertisers cannot use keywords to target users based on the content they interact with or the topics they are interested in. For example, an advertiser promoting a new line of vegan snacks may not target users who are interested in content related to veganism or healthy eating. to eat

Another limitation is that both platforms have limited ability to target users based on their behavior and interests. While Instagram offers some behavioral targeting options, such as targeting users who consume certain types of content or take certain actions on the platform, TikTok's targeting options are much more limited. TikTok only allows advertisers to target based on basic demographic information such as age, gender, location and device type.

Additionally, both platforms have limitations when it comes to targeting users based on their location. While both platforms allow advertisers to target users based on their country, region, or city, they don't offer more specific targeting options like zip code or neighborhood.

Despite these limitations, TikTok and Instagram offer powerful advertising platforms that can help brands reach their target audiences. By focusing on creating engaging and relevant content, advertisers can still connect with their target audience and drive results.

It is important for advertisers to keep these limitations in mind when planning their social media advertising campaigns on TikTok or Instagram. By understanding the limitations of each platform's targeting options, advertisers can set realistic expectations for their campaigns and create strategies that maximize their ROI.

Short video format

As social media continues to dominate the advertising industry, companies are constantly looking for new ways to reach their target audience. One of the most popular methods that has emerged in recent years is the short video format, which can be found on both TikTok and Instagram. In this subsection, we review the pros and cons of this social media advertising format.

The short video format is characterized by brevity, usually between 15 and 60 seconds. This format is especially popular with younger audiences who like fast-paced and visually appealing content. Brands can use short videos to present their products, services or brand personality in a fun and creative way. The format is also great for generating User Generated Content (NGC) by encouraging viewers to participate in challenges or create their own videos.

TikTok's short video format is its primary content mode. The program's algorithm favors videos that are engaging and entertaining, meaning businesses can reach large audiences with a well-crafted video. Instagram's short video feature, Reels, is newer and less established, but offers similar benefits. Reels can be shared on both the Reels tab and the main Instagram feed, giving brands more exposure.

However, the short video format has its drawbacks. Creating a high-quality video can be time-consuming and expensive, especially for small businesses. The brevity of the format also means that brands have limited time to make an impression on viewers. Also, the short video format may not be suitable for all types of products or services. Some businesses may find that longer content, such as blog posts or tutorials, is more effective in communicating their knowledge.

In conclusion, the short video format can be an effective means of advertising on social networks, especially on TikTok and Instagram. However, companies should carefully consider whether this format fits their brand message and target audience. Properly prepared short videos can be an effective way to communicate with customers and increase brand awareness.

Limited analytics

Limited Analytics

One of the biggest challenges in social media marketing is understanding the effectiveness of your campaigns. Both TikTok and Instagram offer analytics to help you measure the success of your advertising, but both have their limitations.

TikTok Analysis

TikTok Analytics is a built-in tool that helps you track your account performance. It provides information about your followers, video views, engagement rates and more. However, TikTok Analytics has some limitations that advertisers should be aware of. First, TikTok Analytics only shows data for the last 7 days. This means you can't track the long-term performance of your campaigns. Second, TikTok Analytics does not provide demographic information such as age, gender, or location. This makes it difficult to understand your target audience and tailor your campaigns accordingly.

Instagram analytics

Instagram Analytics provides many insights into your account's performance, including follower demographics, engagement rates, reach, and impressions. It also allows you to monitor the performance of individual posts and stories.

But even Instagram Analytics has its limitations. First, it only provides data for the last 30 days. This means you can't track the long-term performance of your campaigns. Second, Instagram Analytics does not provide data on the performance of Instagram Reels. This can be a significant limitation for advertisers using scrolls as part of their social media advertising strategy.

Conclusion

While TikTok and Instagram offer analytics to help you measure the success of your ads, both have their limitations. TikTok Analytics only shows data for the last 7 days and does not provide demographic data, while Instagram Analytics only shows data for the last 30 days and does not provide data on the performance of Instagram Reels. As an advertiser, it is very important to be aware of these limitations and apply them to your social media advertising strategy.

Instagram Advertising

Overview of Instagram advertising

Overview of Instagram Advertising

Instagram is a social media platform that has grown exponentially since its inception in 2010. It is now one of the most popular social media platforms with over 1 billion active users worldwide. Instagram advertising is a popular choice for businesses and individuals looking to promote their products or services. In this section, we provide an overview of advertising on Instagram and how it works.

Types of Instagram Ads

Instagram offers several ad formats that businesses can use to reach their target audience. The most common types of Instagram ads are:

1. Photo Ads: These are the most basic Instagram ads that contain a single image with a caption.

2. Video ads: These ads contain a video clip that can last anywhere from a few seconds to a minute.

3. Carousel ads: These ads contain multiple images or videos that users can scroll through.

4. Stories Ads: These ads appear on Instagram Stories and can be a photo or a video.

5. Collection Ads: These ads allow users to browse and purchase products directly from the Instagram app. Application options

Instagram Ads allows businesses to target their ads based on a variety of factors, including demographics, interests, behavior and location. This level of targeting ensures that businesses are reaching the right audience with their ads, increasing engagement and conversion rates.

Price

Instagram advertising costs vary depending on the size of the ad and the level of targeting. Businesses can choose to pay per click, impression or engagement. The cost per click can range from a few cents to several dollars, depending on the competition in the advertising space. Conclusion

Advertising on Instagram provides businesses with many opportunities to reach their target audience. With its large user base and advanced targeting options, Instagram is a popular choice for businesses looking to promote their products or services. Understanding the different ad formats, targeting options, and costs helps businesses create effective Instagram ad campaigns that drive engagement and conversions.

Advantages of Instagram advertising

Instagram advertising has become increasingly popular in recent years, and for good reason. As one of the most widely used social media platforms, Instagram gives businesses the opportunity to reach a large audience and effectively promote their products or services. In this subsection, we'll discuss the benefits of Instagram advertising and why it's a great option for businesses looking to expand their reach.

First, Instagram's user base is huge, with more than a billion active users worldwide. This means that businesses have access to a large audience, making it a great advertising platform. By creating an Instagram business account, businesses can target their desired audience based on demographics, interests and behaviors and ensure that their content is seen by the right people.

Second, Instagram is a visual platform that is ideal for highlighting products or services. High-quality images and videos can be used to promote business offers, and Instagram's various features, such as stories, reels and IGTV, give businesses plenty of opportunities to creatively present their products.

Third, Instagram advertising is cost-effective compared to other advertising channels. Businesses can set a budget for their campaigns, and Instagram's advertising tools give them insights into the performance of their ads so they can adjust their strategy accordingly. Fourth, Instagram has a higher engagement rate than other social media platforms, making it a great platform for businesses to engage with their audience. Instagram's various engagement features, such as comments, likes, and shares, allow businesses to connect and engage with their followers.

Finally, Instagram advertising tools offer businesses many options to effectively promote their offerings. From carousel ads to sponsored posts, businesses can choose the ad type that best suits their goals and audience.

In summary, Instagram ads offer businesses a number of benefits, from a huge user base to cost effectiveness and engagement levels. Effective use of Instagram advertising tools helps businesses reach a wider audience, creatively present their products or services, and build strong relationships with their followers.

Wide range of targeting options

One of the main benefits of social media advertising is the ability to target specific audiences. Both TikTok and Instagram offer a wide range of targeting options to help advertisers reach their desired audience and achieve their marketing goals.

TikTok advertisers can target users based on demographics such as age, gender, and location. They can also target users based on interests, behaviors and device types. For example, an advertiser can target users who have expressed interest in beauty products and are using iOS devices. In addition, TikTok offers custom and lookalike audiences, which allow advertisers to target users who are similar to existing customers or who have interacted with their brand in the past.

Instagram also offers a variety of targeting options, including demographics, interests, behaviors, and location. Advertisers can also target users based on their activity on Instagram, such as whether they like or comment on posts about a certain topic. Instagram also allows advertisers to target users based on their engagement with their activity, such as whether they have used an Instagram profile or visited their website.

Both TikTok and Instagram also offer advanced targeting options such as retargeting and sequential messaging. These options allow advertisers to target users who have already interacted with their brand in some way, such as visiting their website or watching videos.

However, it is important to note that the effectiveness of targeting options depends on the quality of data provided by social media platforms. Advertisers should carefully consider their audience and targeting options to ensure they are reaching the right consumers with the right message.

In conclusion, TikTok and Instagram offer a wide range of targeting options to help advertisers reach their desired audience and achieve their marketing goals. Advertisers should carefully consider their audience and targeting options to ensure they are reaching the right consumers with the right message.

Visual appeal

Visual appeal is one of the most important aspects of advertising on social media platforms like TikTok and Instagram. These platforms are all about visual content, and if your ads don't look good, they won't get the attention they need. In this subsection, we will look at the importance of visual appeal in TikTok and Instagram ads.

First, let's talk about TikTok. TikTok is a platform that revolves around short videos, so your ads need to be visually appealing to grab users' attention. TikTok's unique algorithm means that even if you have a small following, your video can still go viral if it's engaging and visually appealing. You should focus on creating eye-catching videos with vibrant colors and dynamic motion. Use text overlays to emphasize your message and make sure the video is easy to understand without sound, as many users watch TikTok videos on mute.

Instagram, on the other hand, is a platform that revolves around beautiful images. Your ads need to be visually stunning to stand out from the crowd. Instagram is a platform where users find inspiration, so make sure your ads are visually appealing and ambitious. Use high-quality images and videos, and consider using Instagram's various creative tools to make your ads stand out. Instagram Stories is also a big part of the platform, so make sure your ads are optimized for that format as well.

It's important to remember that visual appeal isn't just about making your ads look good. Your ads should be visually appealing and relevant to your target audience. Understand the tastes and preferences of your target audience and create ads that match them. This helps ensure that your ads are effective and deliver the desired results.

In short, visual appeal is a crucial aspect of advertising on both TikTok and Instagram. Whether you're creating short videos for TikTok or beautiful images for Instagram, you need to make sure your ads are visually appealing and engaging. With the right approach, you can create ads that resonate with your target audience and drive the results you're looking for.

Large user base

Large User Base

One of the main advantages of advertising on TikTok and Instagram is the huge user base of both platforms. in 2021 TikTok has more than 1.2 billion active users worldwide, while Instagram has more than 1 billion. Both platforms have mostly young users, with TikTok being more popular with Gen Z and Instagram with millennials.

A large user base means that your ads can reach a large audience. This is especially useful for brands that want to build awareness or introduce new products to a large audience. Plus, high engagement rates on both platforms mean your ads will be seen and used more often by users.

Another advantage of a large user base is the ability to target specific audiences. Both TikTok and Instagram offer advanced targeting options that allow advertisers to target users based on age, location, interests, behavior, and more. This level of targeting ensures that your ads are shown to people who are most likely to be interested in your products or services.

But a large user base also means more competition. With millions of users on both platforms, it can be difficult to stand out and capture the attention of your target audience. This is where creativity and innovation come in. Your ads must be visually appealing, engaging and relevant to your target audience.

Another challenge of advertising on platforms with many users is the risk of getting lost in the noise. With so many users and so much content being created every day, it can be difficult to target your ads to the right people. That's why it's so important to have a clear strategy and constantly monitor and adjust your campaigns to get the best results.

In conclusion, the large user base of TikTok and Instagram gives advertisers a lot of opportunities to reach large audiences and target specific demographics.

But it also brings more competition and the risk of getting lost in the noise. With a clear strategy and visually appealing and relevant ads, you can maximize the potential of these platforms and achieve your advertising goals.

Disadvantages of Instagram advertising

Disadvantages of Instagram Advertising

While Instagram advertising has many advantages, it also has some disadvantages that advertisers should be aware of. In this section, we will discuss some of the disadvantages of Instagram advertising that you should consider before investing your advertising budget.

1. High competition

Instagram is a popular platform for businesses, so competition for advertising space is high. This means your ads can get lost in a sea of other ads, making it difficult for your message to stand out. 2. Advertising fatigue

With so many ads on Instagram, users can quickly tire of seeing them. This can lead to ad fatigue, which means that users start to ignore or even dislike ads, making it difficult for advertisers to reach their target audience.

3. Limited application options

While Instagram offers some targeting options such as geo-targeting and interest-based targeting, these options are not as advanced as other social media platforms. This means that it can be difficult to reach a very specific audience on Instagram.

4. Limited analysis

Compared to other advertising platforms, Instagram analytics is limited. This means that it can be difficult to measure the effectiveness of campaigns and make data-driven decisions.

5. Addiction to visual content

Instagram is a visual platform, which means advertisers need to create visually appealing content to be successful. This can be a disadvantage for companies without strong visual content or in industries that are not visually appealing.

While there are many advantages to Instagram advertising, there are a few disadvantages that advertisers should be aware of. Understanding these drawbacks can help you make informed decisions about whether Instagram ads are right for your business.

High competition

High Competition

One of the biggest challenges businesses face when advertising on social media platforms like TikTok and Instagram is the high level of competition. With millions of businesses competing for the same audience's attention, it can be difficult to stand out and make a lasting impression.

The competition on TikTok is especially fierce. The platform is still relatively new compared to Instagram, and as more businesses use the app, it becomes harder to get noticed. TikTok's algorithm is extremely difficult to crack, and even the best-designed ads can get lost in a sea of user-generated content. Instagram, on the other hand, has been around much longer and has a more established advertising ecosystem. But that doesn't mean it's any less competitive. In fact, with over a billion active users, it is one of the busiest social media platforms. Brands have to work hard to create visually stunning content that grabs the attention of their target audience.

So what can businesses do to stand out in a sea of competition? One strategy is to focus on creating quality content that resonates with your audience. This means investing in creating high-quality photos and videos, but also spending time creating compelling copy that appeals directly to your target audience.

Another way is to use influencer marketing. By partnering with popular social media influencers, brands can tap into their existing audience and reach a larger pool of potential customers. Influencers can help take your brand message to the next level and give your products or services a more authentic and recognizable voice. Ultimately, you need to find creative ways to cut through the noise and leave a lasting impression on your target audience. With the right approach, even the most competitive social media landscape can be successfully navigated, and businesses can see real results from advertising on platforms like TikTok and Instagram.

Low organic reach

Low Organic Reach

One of the biggest challenges brands and businesses face on social media platforms like TikTok and Instagram is low organic reach. Organic reach refers to the number of people who see your posts without any paid advertising. In other words, it's free viewing of your content on the platform.

Unfortunately, organic reach has declined on both TikTok and Instagram in recent years. This is partly due to the algorithms used by these platforms, which prioritize content that users are most likely to interact with. If your content doesn't get enough likes, comments, shares, or saves, it's less likely to be seen by a larger audience.

So what can you do to improve your organic reach on TikTok and Instagram? Here are some tips:

1. Post consistently: The more you post, the more likely you are to reach your audience. Try to post at least once a day on both platforms. 2. Use appropriate hashtags. Hashtags can help your content be discovered by users searching for specific topics or interests. Make sure you use appropriate hashtags in your posts and stories.

3. Engage your audience: Respond to your followers' comments and messages. This shows that you value their engagement and can help build a loyal following.

4. Create Shareable Content – Users are more likely to share content that is entertaining, inspiring, or informative. Focus on creating content that resonates with your audience and encourage them to share it with their friends.

5. Collaborate with other creators: By collaborating with other creators in your niche, you can reach new audiences and gain more followers.

While organic reach on TikTok and Instagram may be declining, paid advertising can help you reach a larger audience. Both platforms offer a variety of advertising options, including sponsored posts, influencer partnerships, and targeted ads. By combining paid and organic strategies, you can maximize your reach and reach your marketing goals on these popular social media platforms.

Cost of advertising

Advertising cost is a very important factor to consider when deciding whether to use TikTok or Instagram for social media advertising. Both platforms have their own unique features that can make them more appealing to different audiences. However, the cost of advertising on each platform is one of the main differences between the two.

The cost of advertising on Instagram is usually higher than on TikTok. Instagram has a larger user base, which means more businesses are competing for ad space. In addition, Instagram's advertising system has been further improved and the platform offers more advanced targeting options. These factors contribute to Instagram's higher advertising costs, making it less affordable for small businesses with limited advertising budgets.

On the other hand, TikTok's advertising costs are generally lower than Instagram's. The platform has a smaller user base but is growing rapidly, making it an attractive option for businesses looking to reach a younger audience. TikTok's advertising system is also fairly new, so competition for ad space is less. This allows businesses to reach a large audience at a lower cost, making TikTok a more affordable platform for small businesses.

It is important to note that the cost of advertising on both platforms varies depending on several factors such as the type of ad, targeting options and placement of the ad. Businesses should carefully consider their advertising goals and budget to determine which platform will provide the best return on investment.

In conclusion, advertising cost is an important factor in choosing TikTok and Instagram social media advertising. Instagram's larger user base and more complex advertising system make it a more expensive option, while TikTok's smaller user base and evolving advertising system offer cheaper advertising options. Ultimately, businesses must weigh the pros and cons of each platform and consider their advertising goals and budgets to determine which platform will deliver the best results.

TikTok vs Instagram Advertising

Comparison of TikTok and Instagram advertising

When it comes to social media advertising, TikTok and Instagram have become two of the most popular platforms for businesses to reach their target audience. While both platforms offer unique features and benefits, there are significant differences between TikTok and Instagram ads that businesses should consider before deciding which platform to use.

One of the main differences between TikTok and Instagram ads is the type of content created and shared on each platform. TikTok is primarily a video-based platform where users can create and share short videos with music or other audio. Instagram, on the other hand, is a more visually oriented platform where users can share photos, videos, and stories. Another difference between TikTok and Instagram ads is the demographics of their respective user bases. TikTok is most popular with a younger audience, with most users between the ages of 16 and 24. Instagram, on the other hand, has a larger user base that includes both young and old users, with most users aged 18 and above. and 34.

When it comes to advertising options, TikTok and Instagram offer a variety of options for businesses. TikTok offers advertising options like in-feed ads, brand endorsements, and sponsored hashtag challenges, while Instagram offers options like photo and video ads, story ads, and carousel ads. In terms of cost, Instagram ads are generally more expensive than TikTok, especially for larger businesses with bigger budgets. However, TikTok is still a new platform and advertising costs may increase as the platform becomes more popular among businesses.

Ultimately, the choice between TikTok and Instagram ads depends on your specific business goals, audience, and budget. Both platforms have unique advantages and disadvantages, so businesses should carefully consider their options before deciding which platform to use for their social media advertising.

Which platform is best for your business?

When it comes to social media advertising, choosing the right platform can affect the success of your business. Two of the most popular business options are TikTok and Instagram. But which is the best choice for your business?

Let's start by talking about TikTok. The platform has quickly become popular among a younger audience with over 800 million active users worldwide. TikTok is known for its short videos and viral challenges that can spread quickly on the platform.

If your business is targeting a younger audience, TikTok can be a great choice for your social media marketing. The platform is ideal for businesses that can create engaging and shareable visual content. However, this may not be the best choice for companies offering products or services that are not valued by the younger generation.

Instagram, on the other hand, is a more established platform with over 1 billion active users worldwide. Instagram is primarily a photo-sharing platform, but it has expanded to include video content. The platform is ideal for companies that want to visually present their products or services.

Instagram is also a great choice for businesses that appeal to people of all ages. The platform has a diverse user base, so you can reach a large audience with your social media ads.

Basically, choosing the right platform for your business depends on your target audience and the content you intend to create. If your business is aimed at a younger audience and you can create engaging visual content, TikTok may be the best choice for your social media marketing. However, if your business targets people of all ages and you want to present your products or services in a visual way, Instagram may be your best bet. Finally, understanding your audience and their preferences is key to making an informed decision.

Case studies of successful TikTok and Instagram campaigns

Case studies of successful TikTok and Instagram campaigns

One of the most effective ways to learn about the power of TikTok and Instagram ads is to look at real-life examples. In this section, we'll show you some of the most successful campaigns on both platforms and show you where they stand out.

Tick tock

1. Chipotle's #GuacDance Challenge

Chipotle's #GuacDance Challenge was a viral sensation that took TikTok by storm. The challenge encouraged users to post videos of themselves dancing to a song about guacamole. The campaign generated more than 250,000 user-generated videos and helped Chipotle gain more than 100,000 new followers on TikTok.

This campaign cleverly used a catchy song and a fun, shareable challenge that tapped into TikTok's love of dance and humor.

2. The NFL's #WeReady campaign

The NFL's #WeReady campaign was a great example of how brands can use TikTok to connect with a younger audience. The campaign featured famous TikTok creators and NFL players dancing to a remix of a classic football song. The #WeReady hashtag has been used on over 45,000 user-generated videos with over 2.6 billion views.

This campaign was able to capitalize on the use of popular TikTok creators and the NFL's willingness to embrace the culture and humor of the platform.

Instagram

1. Airbnb campaign #WeAccept

Airbnb's #WeAccept campaign was a clear response to the US government's 2017 travel ban. The campaign included a video showcasing Airbnb's commitment to diversity and inclusion. The #WeAccept hashtag was used on more than 38,000 user-generated posts, generating more than 7.5 million views.

The success of this campaign was due to the timely response to an important social issue and the strong message of the Airbnb brand.

2. H&M campaign #HMxME

H&M's #HMxME campaign was a great example of using user-generated content to promote a brand. In the campaign, real customers wore H&M products and shared their style on Instagram. The #HMxME hashtag was used on over 100,000 user-generated posts and generated over 3 million views.

What made this campaign successful was its use of real customers and the brand's ability to harness the power of user-generated content.

All these case studies show the power of TikTok and Instagram ads. By creating shareable content, tapping into popular culture and incorporating user-generated content, brands can connect with younger audiences and create campaigns that resonate.

Best Practices for TikTok and Instagram Advertising

How to create effective TikTok and Instagram ads

How to create effective TikTok and Instagram ads

Creating effective TikTok and Instagram ads requires a strategic approach and attention to detail. Here are some tips to help you create compelling ads on these platforms.

1. Know your audience

Before creating an advertisement, it is necessary to understand the target audience. TikTok's user base tends to be younger, with a large percentage of users between the ages of 16 and 24. On the other hand, Instagram's user base is more diverse in terms of age and interests. Knowing your target audience will help you create ads that appeal to them and drive engagement.

2. Keep it short and sweet

Both TikTok and Instagram have short video formats, so it's important to keep your ad concise and relevant. Aim for no more than 15 seconds on TikTok and 30 seconds on Instagram. Use striking visuals and a clear message to grab your audience's attention quickly.

3. Use appropriate hashtags

Hashtags are an important part of TikTok and Instagram and help your content reach a wider audience. Look for hashtags that work for your target audience and include them in your ad copy. This increases the chance that your ad will be seen by users who don't follow your account. 4. Use user-generated content

One of the most effective ways to create advertising that resonates with your target audience is to use user-generated content. This could include reposting customer videos or encouraging them to create content related to your brand. User-generated content can provide a more authentic and relatable perspective, which can increase engagement and increase conversions.

5. Optimize for mobile devices

Both TikTok and Instagram are mobile-first platforms, so optimizing your ads for mobile delivery is critical. Use high-quality images and make sure your ad is easy to view on a small screen. Avoid using small text that is difficult to read on a mobile device.

Basically, creating effective TikTok and Instagram ads requires a thoughtful approach and attention to detail. By understanding your audience, keeping it short and concise, using the right hashtags, using user-generated content, and optimizing for mobile devices, you can create ads that drive engagement and conversions on these popular social media platforms.

Tips for targeting the right audience

When it comes to social media advertising, targeting the right audience is key to the success of your campaign. In this subsection, we provide some tips on how to target the right audience on TikTok and Instagram.

1. Define your target audience: Before starting an advertising campaign, you need to define your target audience. who are they What are their interests? What are their pain points? Once you've defined your target audience, you can tailor your marketing message to their needs and preferences.

2. Use the right hashtags: Hashtags are a great way to target your audience on both TikTok and Instagram. By using relevant hashtags, you increase the visibility of your content and attract the attention of your target audience.

3. Leveraging Influencers: Influencers are a powerful tool to reach your target audience on both TikTok and Instagram. Find influencers in your niche who have a large following and engage with your audience. Work with them to promote your products or services. 4. Use Geo-Targeting: Geo-targeting allows you to target your audience based on their location. This is especially useful if you have a local business or want to target a specific region or country.

5. Use Retargeting: Retargeting allows you to target people who are already interested in your brand. For example, if someone visited your website or engaged with your content on social media, you can retarget ads on TikTok or Instagram.

6. Test and Optimize: Finally, it is important to test and optimize your TikTok and Instagram ad campaigns. Track results and adjust your targeting, messaging and ads to improve your performance.

By following these tips, you will be able to target the right audience on TikTok and Instagram and achieve your advertising goals. Remember that social media advertising is about connecting with your target audience, so take the time to understand their needs and preferences and tailor your marketing message accordingly.

Measuring the success of your campaigns

Measuring the success of your campaigns is critical to ensuring that your efforts are not wasted. When creating campaigns for TikTok or Instagram, you should have a clear idea of what you want to achieve. It can drive traffic to your website, increase brand awareness or drive sales.

To measure the success of your TikTok or Instagram campaigns, you should track the following metrics:

1. Reach: Refers to the number of people who have viewed your content. The greater the reach, the more effective your campaign will be.

2. Engagement: Includes likes, comments, shares and saves. A higher engagement rate shows that your content is resonating with your audience.

3. Click-through rate (CTR): Measures the number of clicks on your ad compared to the number of impressions. Show how effective your ad is in driving traffic to your website.

4. Conversions: This refers to the number of people who take a desired action, such as filling out a form or making a purchase. Indicate the success of the campaign in achieving its objectives. In addition to these metrics, you can also analyze target location demographics such as age, gender, location, and more. This helps you create more targeted campaigns and improve ROI.

Both TikTok and Instagram offer analytics tools that help you track these stats. You can also use third-party tools like Hootsuite, Buffer, or Sprout Social for more detailed information.

In short, measuring the success of your TikTok or Instagram campaigns is essential to optimizing your marketing efforts and achieving your goals. Tracking the right metrics and analyzing data will help you make informed decisions and create more effective campaigns in the future.

Conclusion

Recap of the pros and cons of TikTok and Instagram advertising

Recap of the Pros and Cons of TikTok and Instagram Advertising

In this section, we look at the pros and cons of advertising on two of today's most popular social media platforms: TikTok and Instagram. Each platform has its own unique features and advantages, as well as disadvantages and limitations, so it is important to weigh the pros and cons before investing time and money in advertising.

Advantages of TikTok:

1. Huge reach: With over 1 billion active users, TikTok is one of the fastest growing social media platforms. This means that you have the opportunity to reach a large audience. 2. High engagement: TikTok's algorithm favors content that drives high engagement, so if your ad is well-received, it can go viral and get a lot of views.

3. Creative Freedom: TikTok's short video format allows a lot of creative freedom, which can be a great way to show your brand personality and connect with your audience.

Disadvantages of TikTok:

1. Limited targeting: TikTok's targeting options aren't as robust as other platforms, so it can be difficult to reach specific audiences.

2. Limited ad formats: TikTok currently only offers a few ad formats, which may limit your creativity and options when creating ads.

3. User Demographics: TikTok's user base is largely comprised of a younger audience, which may not suit all brands. Advantages of Instagram:

1. Targeting Options: Instagram offers many targeting options including location, interests, behavior, etc., making it easier to reach your desired audience.

2. Ad formats: Instagram offers a variety of ad formats, including photos, videos, carousels, and stories. This gives you more opportunities to present your brand.

3. User Demographics: Instagram has a large user base that spans all age groups, making it a great platform to reach a diverse audience.

Disadvantages of Instagram:

1. High competition: With so many brands advertising on Instagram, it can be difficult to stand out and get your message across.

2. Ad Fatigue: Instagram users are constantly bombarded with ads, which can lead to ad fatigue and reduced engagement. 3. Limited organic reach: Instagram's algorithm favors paid content over organic content, which will make it harder to reach your audience without investing in advertising.

Bottom line: TikTok and Instagram offer unique advantages and disadvantages when it comes to advertising. When deciding which platform to invest in, it's important to consider your audience, creative goals, and budget. Understanding the pros and cons of each platform will help you make an informed decision that will help you achieve your advertising goals.

Final thoughts on choosing the right platform for your business

In short, choosing the right platform for your business is crucial to achieving your advertising goals. Both TikTok and Instagram offer unique social media advertising opportunities and benefits, but which one you choose will depend on your business goals, audience, and budget.

Before choosing a platform, research and understand the platform's demographics, features, and advertising capabilities. Keep in mind that TikTok is a relatively new platform and its user base is mostly made up of younger generations, while Instagram has a more diverse user base that includes both younger and older generations.

Consider your target audience and their preferences when choosing a platform. If your target audience is primarily Gen Z and Millennials, then TikTok might be for you. However, if your audience is more diverse and includes members of an older generation, Instagram may be a better fit for your audience.

Budget is also a very important factor when choosing a platform. TikTok may have lower advertising costs than Instagram, but it also offers limited targeting options. Instagram, on the other hand, offers more advanced targeting options, but it may come at a higher price. Ultimately, the key to success on social media is creating engaging and relevant content that resonates with your target audience. No matter which platform you choose, be sure to track your results and adjust your strategy as needed to meet your advertising goals.

In conclusion, whether you choose TikTok or Instagram for your social media ads, be sure to do your research, understand your target audience, and create compelling content that resonates with them. With the right strategy and execution, both platforms can be invaluable tools for growing your business and reaching new customers.

Recommendations for future social media advertising strategies

In today's digital age, social media has become an ever-expanding platform for businesses to promote their products and services. As the world's focus shifts from traditional marketing strategies to social media advertising, it's critical to be well-versed in digital marketing best practices and current trends. With the rise of the TikTok and Instagram platforms, it is critical to determine which platform is most effective for social media marketing based on your business goals. Here are some recommendations for future social media advertising strategies based on the pros and cons of TikTok and Instagram ads.

First, it's important to understand the demographics of each platform. While TikTok is more popular with a younger audience, Instagram has a wider age range. Depending on your target audience, you can choose which platform works best for your business.

Second, make sure your content is relevant and engaging. Both TikTok and Instagram have different types of content that resonate with their users. While TikTok is known for its short videos, Instagram is great for visual content like images and videos. When creating content, make sure it's tailored to the platform and audience you're targeting.

Third, it is very important that your content has a clear call to action. Whether they visit your website, download an app, or buy a product, your call to action needs to be clear and concise.

Fourth, consider partnering with influencers on both platforms. Influencer marketing has proven to be an effective way to reach a larger audience. However, making sure the influencer aligns with your brand values and message is critical.

Finally, monitor your results and adjust your strategy accordingly. Social media advertising is an ever-changing landscape, so it's imperative to keep up with the latest trends and developments. Analyze your data regularly and adjust your strategy as needed to ensure you're getting the most out of your social media advertising efforts.

In short, TikTok and Instagram are great social media advertising platforms, each with their own pros and cons. Understanding demographics, creating engaging content, clear calls to action, partnering with influencers and tracking results will help you create an effective social media advertising strategy on any platform.

Appendix: Glossary of Terms

Definitions of key terms used throughout the book

To properly understand the pros and cons of TikTok and Instagram ads, it's important to first understand the key terms used in this book. The following are definitions of some key terms that will be used in these chapters:

1. Social Media Advertising: It is the practice of using social media platforms to promote and sell products or services.

2. TikTok Ads: TikTok Ads are a type of social media ads that promote products or services on the TikTok platform. This can include sponsored content, influencer marketing and paid advertising.

3. Instagram Ads: Instagram ads are a form of social media advertising that promotes products or services on the Instagram platform. This can include sponsored content, influencer marketing and paid advertising.

4. Sponsored Content: Sponsored content is content created or shared by an influencer or brand in exchange for compensation. These can be social media posts, videos or blog posts.

5. Influencer Marketing: Influencer marketing is a form of marketing that leverages the influence of popular social media users to promote products or services. This could be sponsored content or other forms of collaboration. 6. Paid Ads: Paid ads are ads that are paid for by a brand or an advertiser. These can be text ads, image ads, or video ads.

7. Engagement: Engagement refers to the level of interaction a social media post receives. This can include likes, comments, shares and other forms of engagement.

By understanding these basic concepts, readers will be able to better understand the nuances and intricacies of TikTok and Instagram advertising. In the following sections, we will examine the pros and cons of each platform and provide useful information for social media advertisers.

References

List of sources cited throughout the book

As a comprehensive guide to the world of social media advertising, Pros and Cons of TikTok and Instagram Ads: A Must-Read for Everyone offers a wealth of information and insight for anyone looking to get the most out of these powerful platforms. Throughout the book, the authors draw on a variety of sources to support their arguments and help readers better understand the dynamics of social media advertising.

To enable readers to explore these resources in more detail, the book provides an extensive list of citations organized by chapter and topic. This list includes academic research, industry reports, and case studies from a variety of sources, giving readers a variety of perspectives on the pros and cons of TikTok and Instagram ads.

Some of the main sources cited in the book are:

- Pew Research Center's Social Media Fact Sheet summarizing the demographics of social media users and the types of content they interact with across all platforms. This research is used to support arguments about the importance of targeting and personalization in social media advertising.

- eMarketer report on TikTok's advertising growth in the US, highlighting the platform's potential to reach younger audiences and increase brand awareness. This report is used to support arguments about the unique advantages of TikTok ads over other platforms.

- Journal of Advertising Research study on the effectiveness of Instagram influencer marketing, which examines the impact of sponsored posts on consumer attitudes and purchase intentions. This research is used to support arguments about the value of influencer marketing as an audience engagement strategy on Instagram. - Hootsuite case study of a successful TikTok ad campaign for fashion brand Guess, demonstrating the potential of leveraging the platform to promote user-generated content and drive engagement. This case study is used to illustrate the practical application of the strategies discussed in the book.

The list of resources mentioned in Pros and Cons of TikTok and Instagram Ads provides readers with a wealth of information and insights to help them better understand the opportunities and challenges of social media advertising. Whether you're a marketer, entrepreneur, or just interested in the world of social media, this book is an essential resource for navigating the rapidly changing landscape of digital advertising.